AF531156

V A N G O G H

I N

P O E M S

Carol Dine

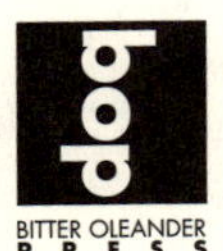

The Bitter Oleander Press
2009

The Bitter Oleander Press
4983 Tall Oaks Drive
Fayetteville, New York 13066-9776
USA

www.bitteroleander.com
info@bitteroleander.com

First Edition

ISBN# 0-9786335-2-0

Library of Congress Control Number: 2008940088

Extreme gratitude is owed The Metropolitan Museum of Art in New York, The Van Gogh Museum (Vincent van Gogh Foundation), Amsterdam and the Kröller-Müller Museum of Otterlo, The Netherlands for their kind permission to incorporate all of the Vincent van Gogh drawings included here.

Cover Layout by *assante design, inc.*
Syracuse, NY 13204

Photograph on back cover of Carol Dine by Arthur Furst
Public Garden with Fence (detail in background) courtesy of The Van Gogh Museum (Vincent van Gogh Foundation), Amsterdam.

Printed by McNaughton & Gunn, Inc.
Saline, Michigan 48176-0010

Manufactured in the United States of America

This book would have been merely a sepia dream were it not for the generosity of spirit and resources from the following:

At the Vincent van Gogh Museum, Amsterdam: Esther Hoofwijk, Saskia Beukers-Jacobs, Ellen Jansen, Marije Vellekoop, Marije Wissink and Roelie Zwikker; the Kröller-Müller Museum, Otterlo, The Netherlands: Margaret Nab; and the Metropolitan Museum of Art: Jeri Wagner. I am grateful for the support of the Saint Botolph Club Foundation, President David Sargent of Suffolk University, as well as Dean Kenneth Greenberg, Dr. Anthony Merzlak, William Davis, and Peter Rubie, my agent. The critiques of my writing group, Jennifer Barber, Linda Cutting, C.D. Collins and Pam Bernard have been so valuable, as has the time we have spent over the years at Wellspring House. And always my gratitude to my dear friends and family: SoHyun Bae, Andrzej Jackowski, Tehila Lieberman, Hilary Nanda and Susan Sullivan; Laura Dine Aaronson, David Aaronson, John Levy, Shirley Levy and to my mother, Estelle Dine. Their acceptance of me as an artist has made possible my life's work.

CONTENTS

DESCENT

NATURE

PLATES

UNEXPECTED MUSE
An Introduction

I had nothing left to say. It was the beginning of summer, and I'd just moved into a new apartment. I began poems, one more trite than the next. My language was dried up, empty. I don't know why I crossed the room to my bookcase. On the bottom shelf, an oversized book my sister had bought for me after an exhibition we'd attended. "Van Gogh: An Appreciation of his Art." It seemed to open to the painting *Almond Blossom.*

My spirits lifted at first sight of the flowering branches. I thought of a bride dancing under a turquoise sky. I looked closer. The blossoms were not pure white. They were tinged with pale green; some had withered. The branches did not entwine but gnarl. With Van Gogh as muse, I began a poem about the beauty and agony of love.

I knew only the basics about the artist's tortured life, his posthumous fame. He liked to paint sunflowers. The popular *Starry Night* was reproduced on posters and refrigerator magnets. The next morning, I hurried to the bookstore. From a shelf devoted to him, I picked up a paperback: "Dear Theo: The Artist's Intimate Letters to his Brother." On the cover, a self-portrait that both drew me toward it and frightened me: Van Gogh's demonic eyes, his scruffy red beard, the swirling lines of the background, so dizzying that, for a moment, I had to look away.

I found the letters filled with contradictions for what they said about the artist, and what they didn't say. They reveal Van Gogh as an astute observer of nature, as a critic of his own art, as a man with a tattered soul. Sometimes, he is factual. He writes to Theo: "I need money badly, and must repair both my health and my painting box." Sometimes, in despair: "…as a result of this last terrible attack there is hardly any very definite desire…left in my mind." Or triumphant: "Finally, there is a cypress with a star." The letters often move from subject to subject, with no transition. Unlike with his paintings, he does not dwell in his subconscious.

I study *The Garden of Saint-Paul Hospital*, the asylum where Van Gogh had been committed. Words come: "maniacal garden," "bruised sky." Now I'm in a trance, outside time. The poem ends: "I rush back/through my green window." Suddenly, I realize I'm no longer the narrator. I am writing in his voice.

I'm often asked, Why Van Gogh? I've published essays and poems on such artists as Frida Kahlo, Mary Cassatt and Jim Dine, but my relationship to Van Gogh was different from the beginning. I experienced the artist and the man from the inside. Without sounding melodramatic, I identify with Van Gogh's themes: conflagrations with his father, loneliness, financial difficulty, the struggle for recognition. I know the dark tunnel where Van Gogh's spells carried him. I've had my own desperate times. Nor am I a stranger to illness; I've had breast cancer. His words: "My own work, I am risking my life for it" resonate.

My book took me three times to Amsterdam where I was able to study the original Van Gogh's. Paper in hand, in the Van Gogh Museum I pulled my chair up to the recessed glass so I could see clearly *Portrait of the Artist's Mother*. Tourists circled around me. A guard approached. "Madame," he said, "to be this close is not allowed." I was in Amsterdam when the news broke — an X-ray by a researcher at Boston's Museum of Fine Arts revealed Van Gogh's long lost painting *Wild Vegetation* under another painting. In response to the story, the Van Gogh Museum displayed the archived drawing, *Wild Vegetation*, for public viewing.

I've also had private sessions with Van Gogh. Beneath the Museum galleries, white metal grates open like in a bank vault. Another set of grates. I follow the curator to a desk on the far side of a cool empty room. "No pen, please," she says. I take out my pencil and yellow pad. A man who wears white cotton gloves brings a drawing, places it before me. As if on a silver tray, champagne and strawberries! I stare into horizontal shapes that appear and disappear, lines intersecting shadows, smudges of charcoal. I take furious notes, then tentatively raise my hand. He returns, removes the drawing, matted and covered with opaque paper. Silently, he comes with another drawing, and another.

On my third visit to the Museum, I feel like a dignitary. The curator has assembled the drawings I'd requested. However, there were several not on my list. She turns a drawing over. On the other side, the image I'd been looking for, *Studies of a Dead Sparrow*. "Van Gogh often ran out of paper," she says, smiling. The bird floats in sepia across the page. "Do you happen to have *The Garden of Daubigny*?" I ask. She leads me into an adjacent room. In the center of a large, wooden table rests a small book. "Vincent's sketchbook," she says, "I never get to show it." Made of canvas, it's flecked in black and white. Attached to the cover, a tiny piece of suede curls like a pinkie finger. I begin to weep. She pulls on white cotton gloves. Gently, she opens the thick, tanning pages to *The Garden*. The lines fade into the margin. "This is holy," I whisper and bow my head.

— Carol Dine, 2008

For Paul B. Roth: My Theo

For years, art scholars searched for Van Gogh's painting *Wild Vegetation in the Mountains*, a match to the drawing. In 2007, a chance X-ray of Van Gogh's painting *Ravine* at Boston's Museum of Fine Arts revealed the sought-after painting hidden underneath.

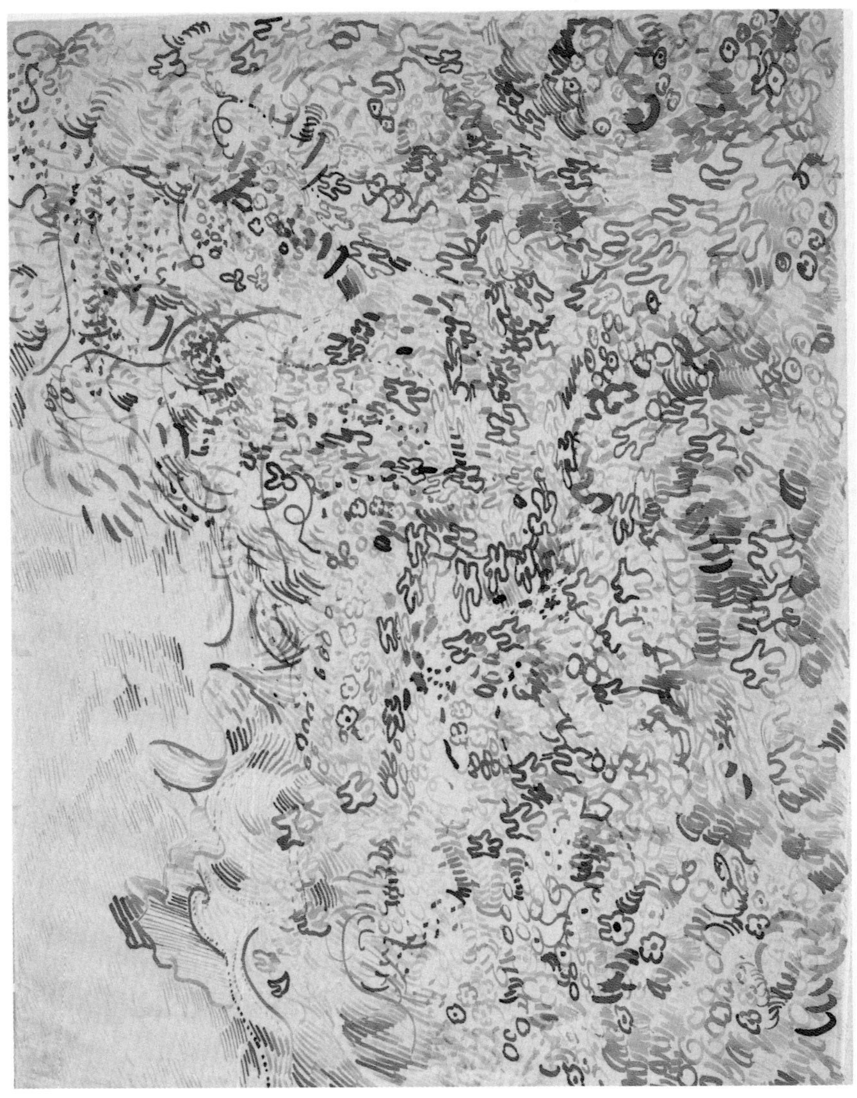

PLATE # 1

Wild Vegetation in the Mountains

Van Gogh Museum, Amsterdam
(Vincent van Gogh Foundation)

VAN GOGH IN POEMS

Carol Dine

FAMILY

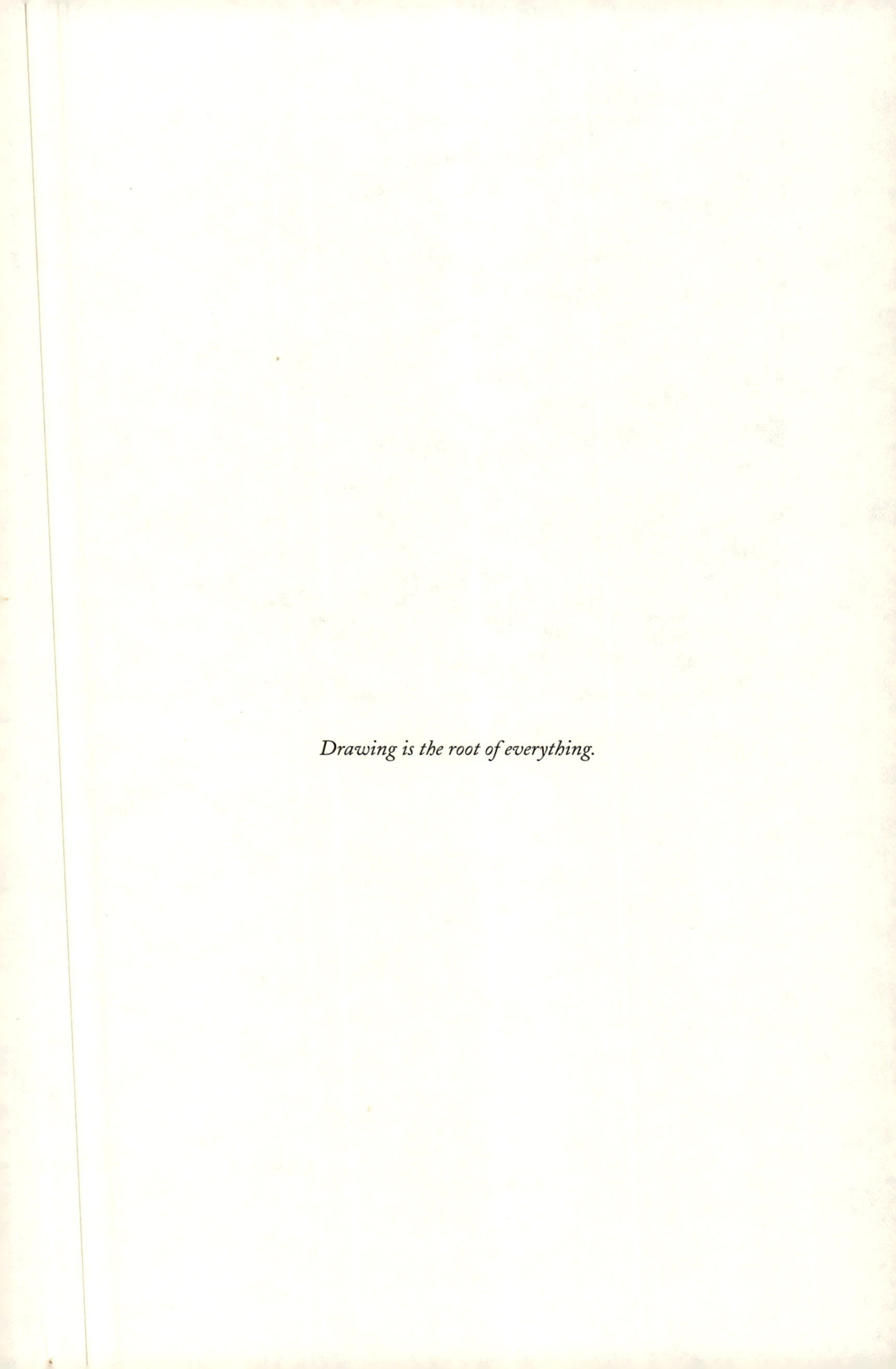

Drawing is the root of everything.

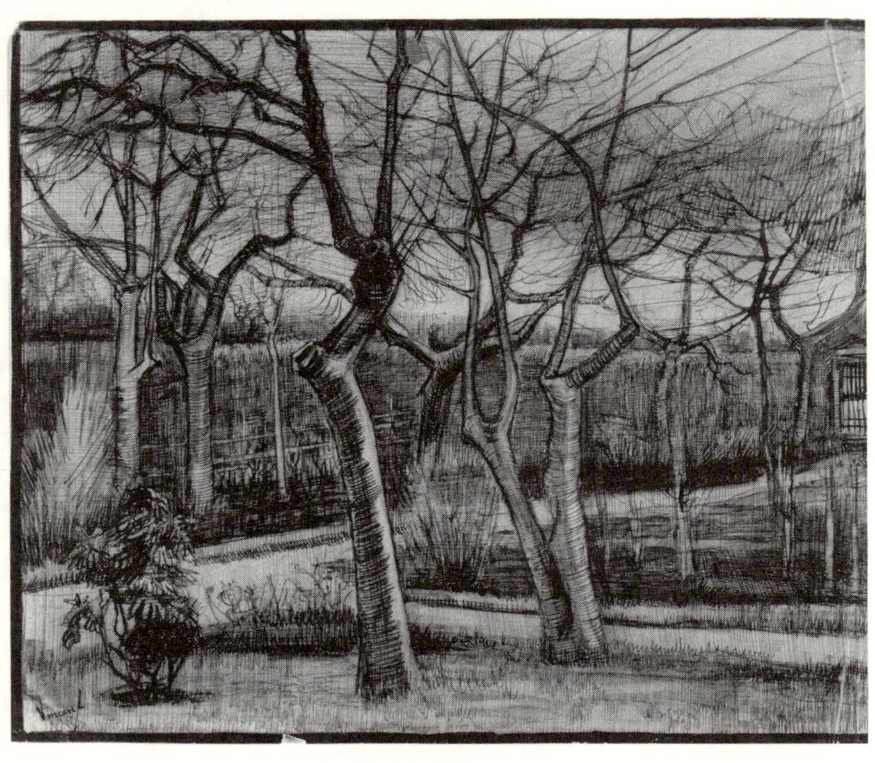

PLATE # 2

The Vicarage Garden

Van Gogh Museum, Amsterdam
(Vincent van Gogh Foundation)

THE VICARAGE GARDEN

Wind agitates the pencil lines,
the fragile web
connecting my family:

Reverend Theodorus
Anna Carbentus

Anna Cornelia
Elisabeth Huberta
Willemina Jacoba
Cornelius Vincent

Vincent Willem.
Named for Mother's
stillborn son,
I draw a nest
in the wound of the bark.

My pen blackens the pollard roots.
Younger brother, Theo,
pays for the ink.

STILL LIFE WITH FIVE BIRDNESTS

Basket of charred potatoes

Headless owl

The womb, blackened, stillborn

Thorned head, pinioned arms,
his mouth, wide open

A red egg
bejeweling the ground

AVENUE OF POPLARS AT SUNSET

Dear Theo: You think that when the shadows are dark, ay, black, it is all wrong.

The end of autumn. I oil the ordinary poplars,
tall and spindly beside the house of our childhood.
I spatter in a few umber and yellow leaves.

Against the rules, the sun has fallen
orange and low into a wooded brush.

Now breaking from the palette: black,
cloaked and moving of its own accord down the path
through the landscape. Black that steals green from the trees.

Consider this: the sunset cannot be beautiful
without the hooded figure that wrestles it,
the figure darker than itself,
darker than the night.

THE VICARAGE AT NUENEN

There is a certain hardness in Father, like iron, an icy coldness.

Father's twilight breeds
beneath the upstairs shades, downstairs,
behind symmetrical, parted curtains.
I study the poplar leaves;
he has siphoned their gold.

THEODORUS VAN GOGH

Your massive black coat,
the upheaval of chins,
the evil that enters your eye slits;
something spawns in your ear canal.
Father, you are a sculpture
I should place on a pedestal.

PORTRAIT OF THE ARTIST'S MOTHER

Close up;
no distance between us.

Your upper lip,
a scratch of red,
your nose, like mine,
a field turnip.

Green birds
have nested on your bonnet.
Creases in your neck appear
to give way.

In your stiffened
burgundy robe,
you outlive three sons
and a husband.
Your eyes ablaze,
malachite.

ALMOND BLOSSOM

I should have greatly preferred Theo to call the boy after Father, instead of after me, but I started right away to make a picture for him.

I cleansed the sky
a double shade of blue.
The blossoms floated.

My apologies, nephew.
On thorny branches,
the off-white petals
turned a sickly green.

I wrapped the buds,
your tiny fists,
in roseate light.

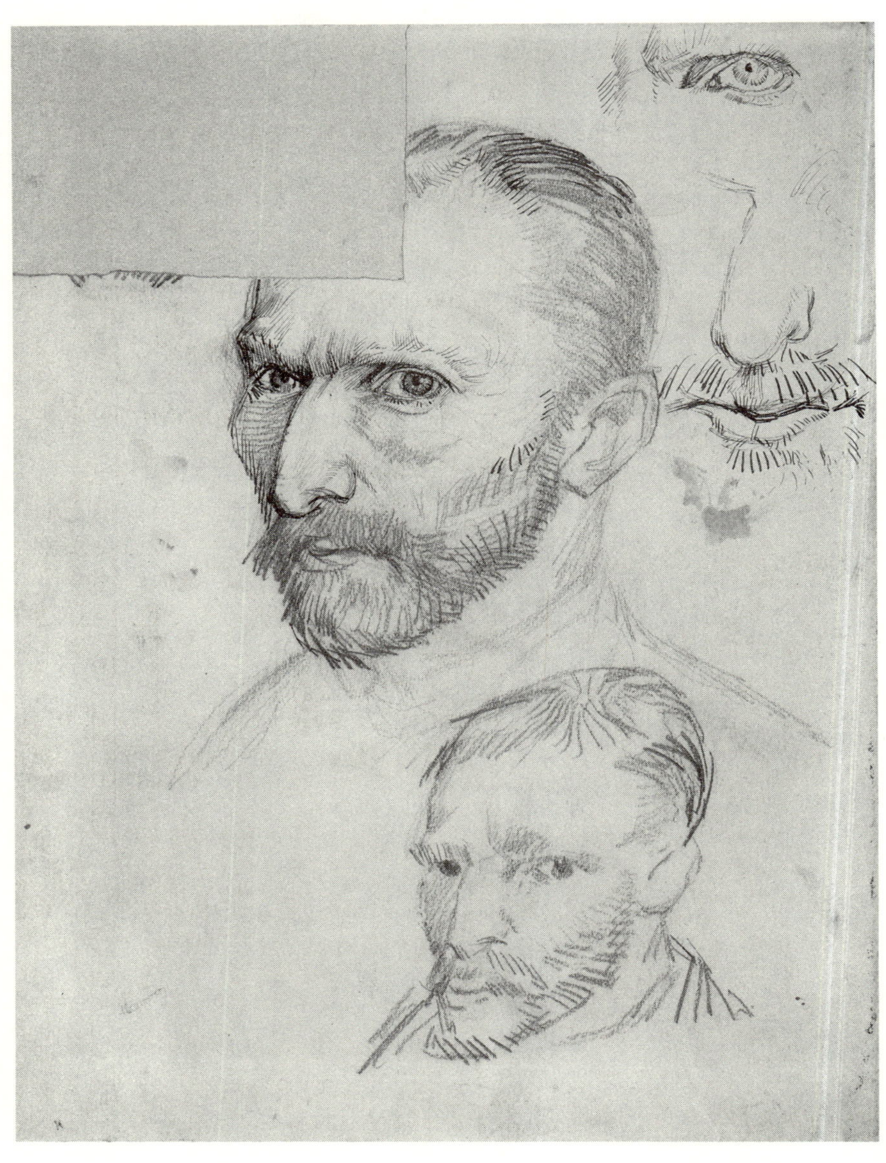

PLATE # 3

Self-Portraits

Van Gogh Museum, Amsterdam
(Vincent van Gogh Foundation)

SELF-PORTRAITS

And then I will take myself off somewhere down south, to get away from the sight of so many painters that disgust me as men.

My features, voices, amplified, floating.
The nose, a phallus at rest. Around the bend
of brow, another brow forms a cliff.

Primitive circles, my eyes
stalk afternoon shadows.

Barbed wire beard;
demonic lines scratch at my cheek.

Seen through the paper,
absence retains its form.

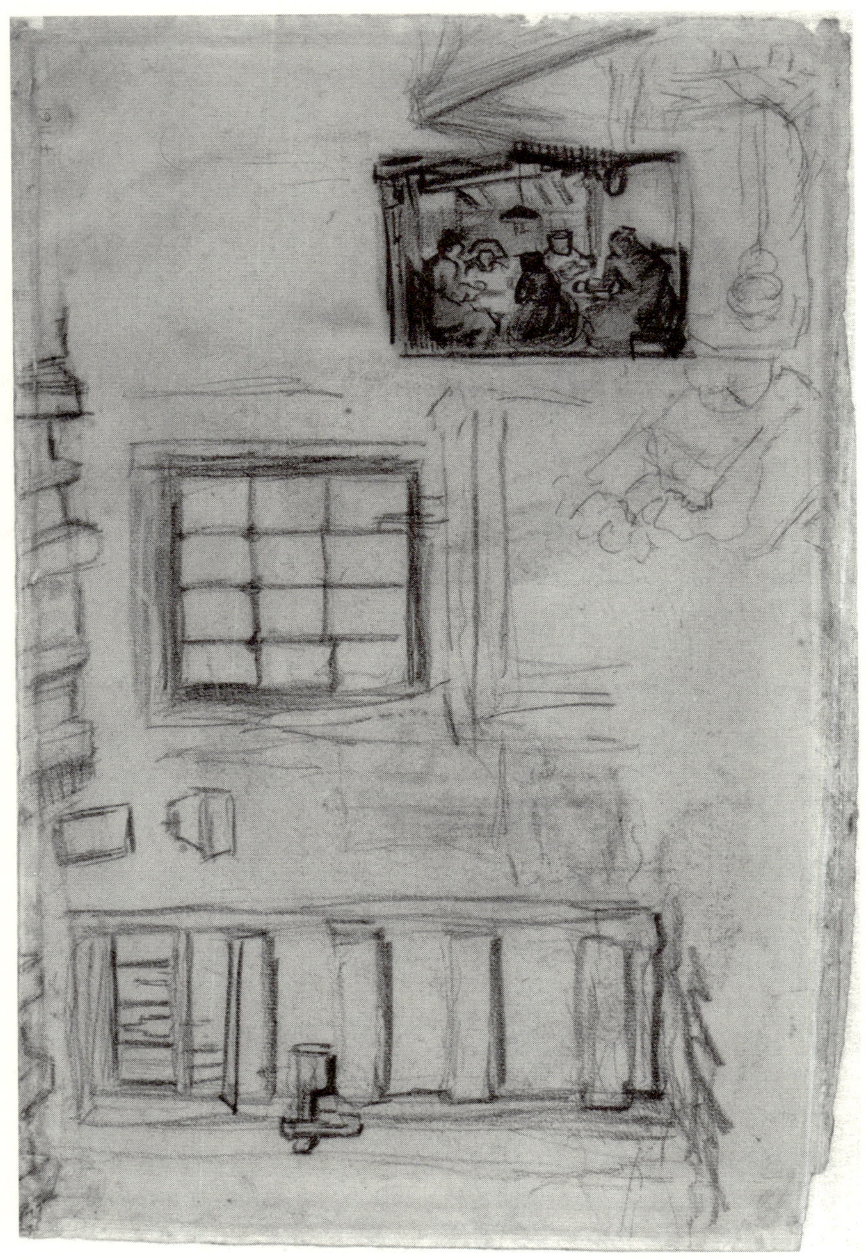

PLATE # 4

Studies of the Interior of a Cottage
and a sketch of "The Potato Eaters"

Van Gogh Museum, Amsterdam
(Vincent van Gogh Foundation)

STUDY OF A COTTAGE

All that I need:

bolted door
black chalk
a bowl of potatoes.

RELIGION

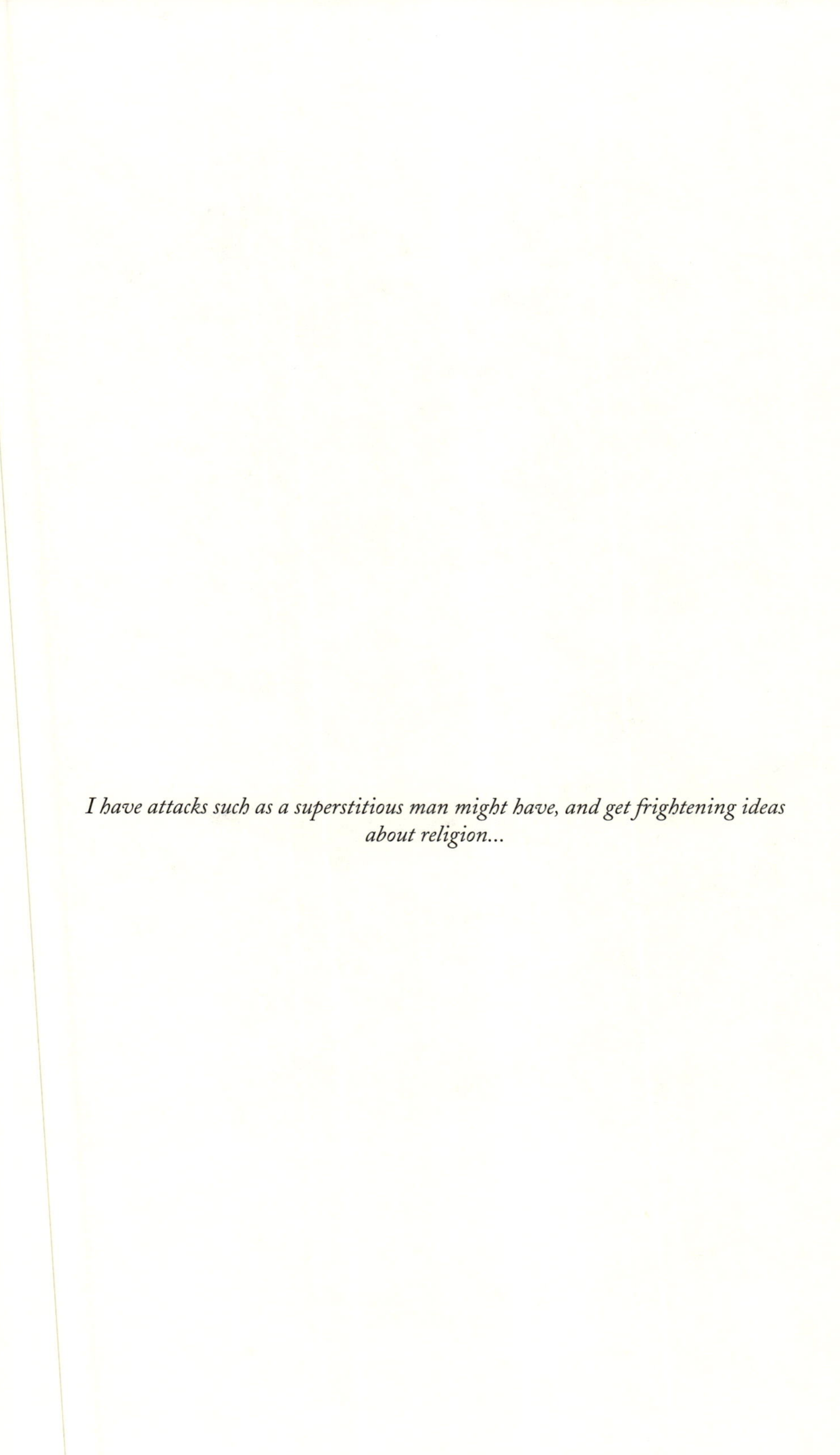

I have attacks such as a superstitious man might have, and get frightening ideas about religion...

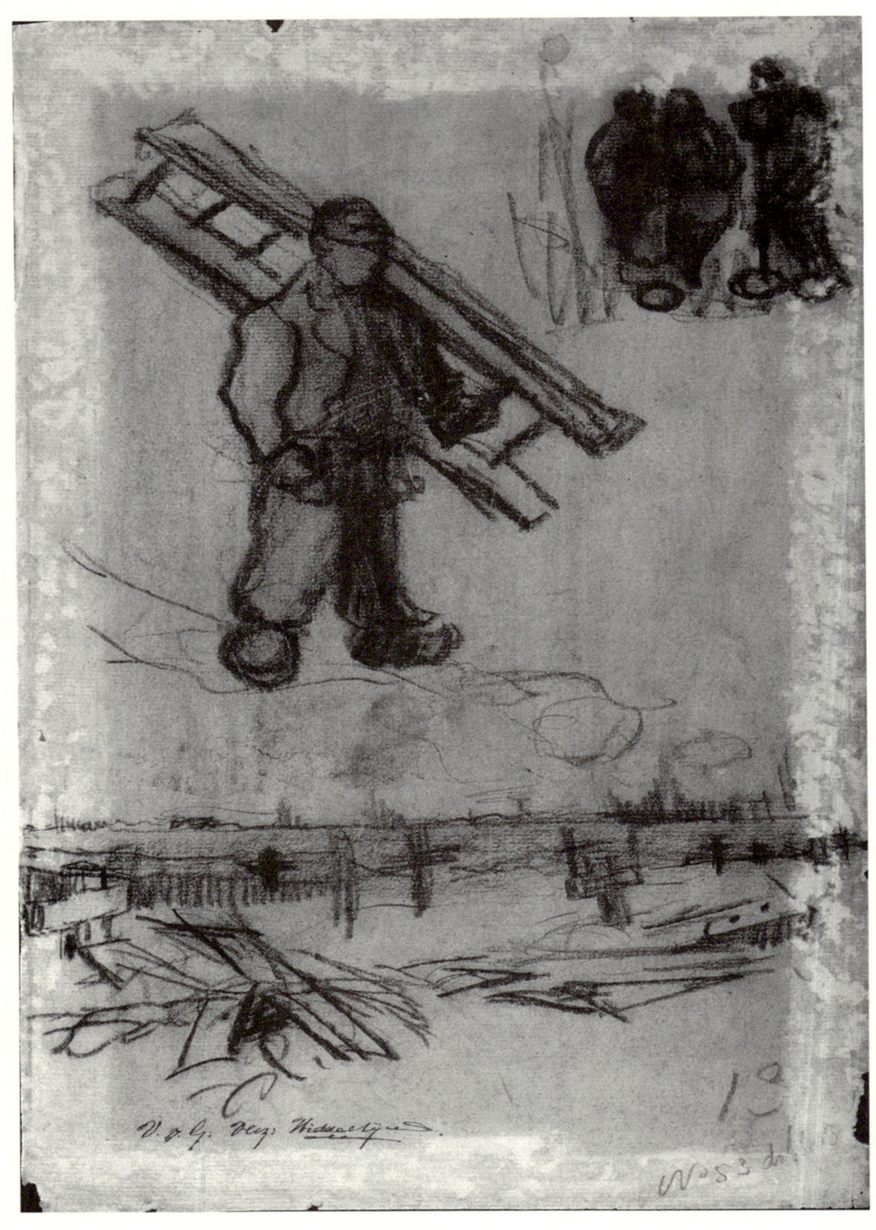

PLATE # 5

Man with Ladder

*Collection Kröller-Müller Museum,
Otterlo, The Netherlands*

MAN WITH LADDER

Thunder inside my head:
my easel, a ladder
I shoulder through fields
in Arles.

In the church's doorway,
three jeering men.
I am rising through smoke.
Below,

        my canvases in a pyre   scattered crosses
            a black crow

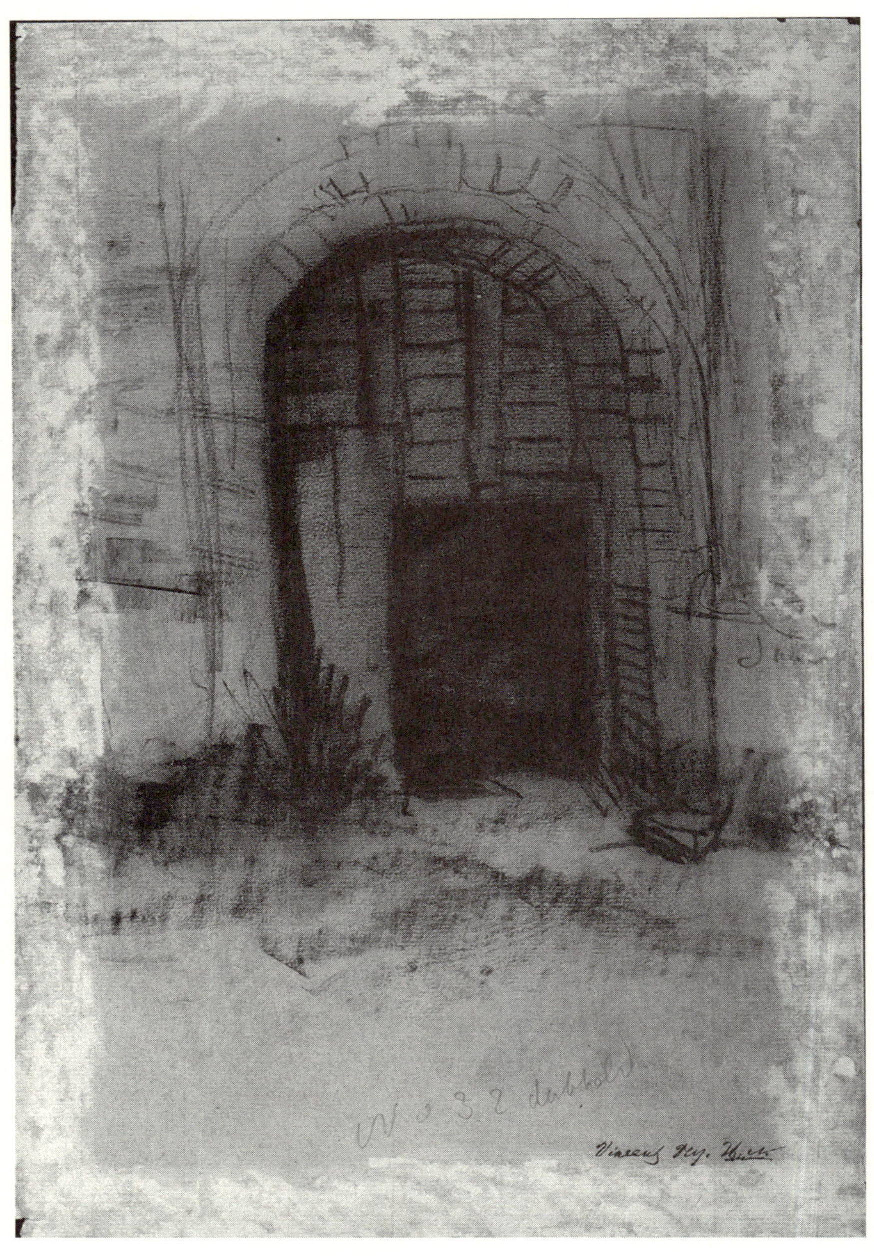

PLATE # 6

An Old Port

Collection Kröller-Müller Museum,
Otterlo, The Netherlands

AN OLD PORT

Through the slatted arch,
black chalk
on the floor
of the tomb.

In the light
outside,
fronded palms;
a kneeling
marked on the grass.

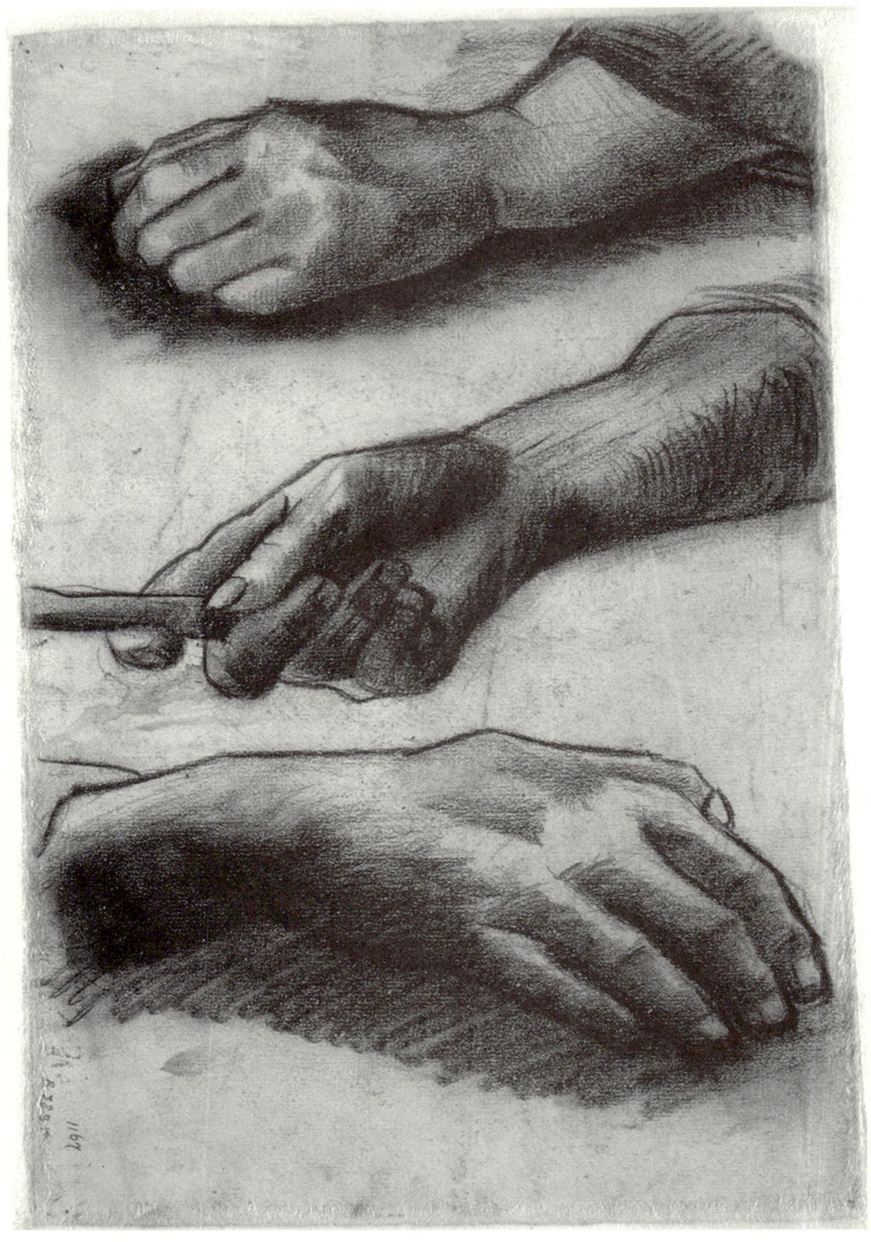

PLATE # 7

Study of Three Hands

Van Gogh Museum, Amsterdam
(Vincent van Gogh Foundation)

THREE HANDS

In the shadows,
fingers engorged
like tubers.

The calloused hand
gives up
the brush.

Escaped from the sleeve,
light finds its way
to the reluctant knuckle.

PIÈTA

(after Delacroix)

Moon rings veil her eyes.
He is draped in sunset.

A mountain, bluing,
she hems him to the grotto.

His chest, his arm, overgrown
ivy.

The landscape rises
without him.

THE PRISONERS' ROUND

Circle of the damned; our skin turns green.
Beneath our boots, the floor is greased
shadow.

A young man's bare head is anointed.
On its hands and knees,
blue light scales the brick wall.

PORTRAIT OF EUGÈNE BOCH

Poet
his shoulders slope

from the weight
of the velvet blue sky.

His cheekbones, ridged
like pink mountains.

The stars are droplets
of paint.

Oh, to capture his eyes

like drifting
souls.

THE NIGHT CAFÉ

The picture… one of the ugliest I have done.

Drunk, the scattered faithful bow their heads;
the floor tilts, absinthe yellow.

Café walls stained
the red of poppies;

the altar, the bar
putrid green.

Midnight; a tolling
from the oil lamps,

concentric circles
of gold.

A presence in the doorway
exhaling light.

The devil shimmers
in the mirror on the wall.

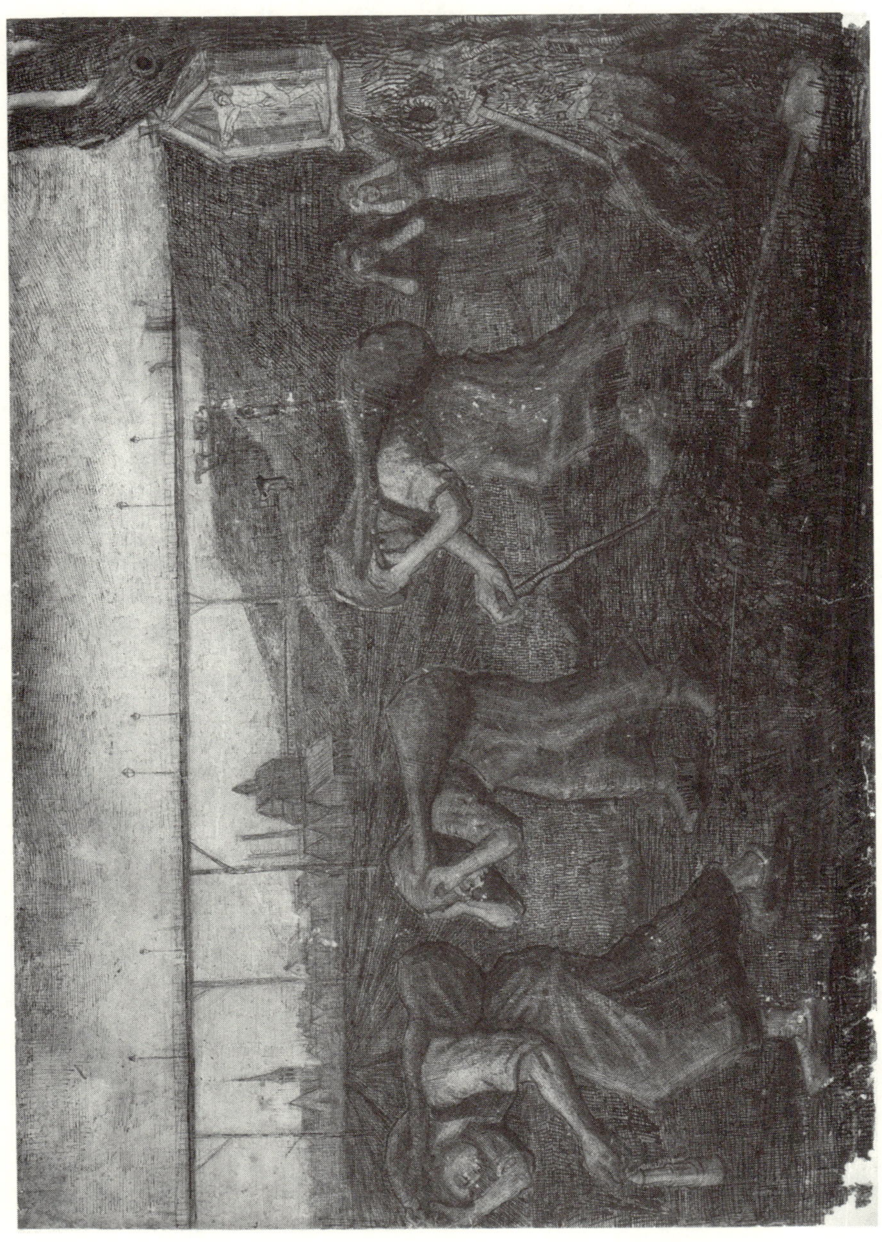

PLATE # 8

The Bearers of the Burden

Collection Kröller-Müller Museum,
Otterlo, The Netherlands

THE BEARERS OF THE BURDEN

Sleepwalking,
the miners pass through the valley,
the shadows of blackthorn hedges.

Discarded shovel.
Christ suspended in a tree,
a bird with useless wings.

What they carry
is rounded to their backs,
spilling itself as diamond light.

THE CHURCH AT AUVERS-SUR-OISE

Waves of greenery
levitate the church.

My beard unfurls
on the orange roof.

Soles of my worn-out shoes
moving uphill in terrible need.

Heaven has never seen
such a pure cobalt sky.

I climb the spire to bellow
my name.

STILL-LIFE WITH OPEN BIBLE

Its pages blurred, pastel,
the family Bible, oversized prop
at the back of the table.

In full sorrel light,
Zola's *La Joie de Vivre*
I had pulled from its binding,
devoured
to the last words:

"How can one be so stupid
as to kill oneself!"

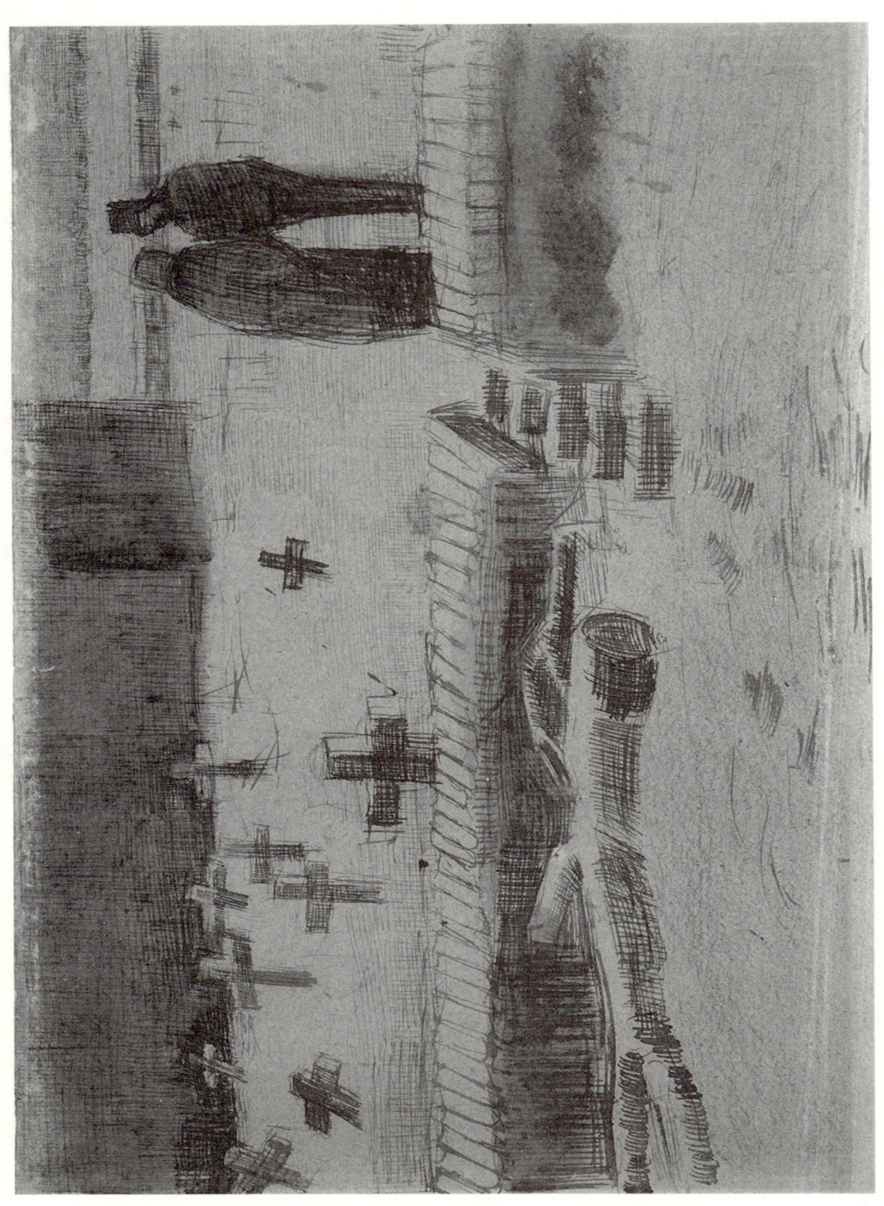

PLATE # 9

Churchyard in Winter

Van Gogh Museum, Amsterdam
(Vincent van Gogh Foundation)

CHURCHYARD IN WINTER

On the ground, a torso
turned to lumber.

Five steps up to heaven,
a frozen lake.

Crosses straining
to hold out their arms;
the city, cordoned off.

Hurry to the conductor.
Ask directions.

L O V E

As for ever having a wife of my own, I have no great faith in that. I am too old to go back on my steps. That desire has left me, though the mental suffering from it still remains.

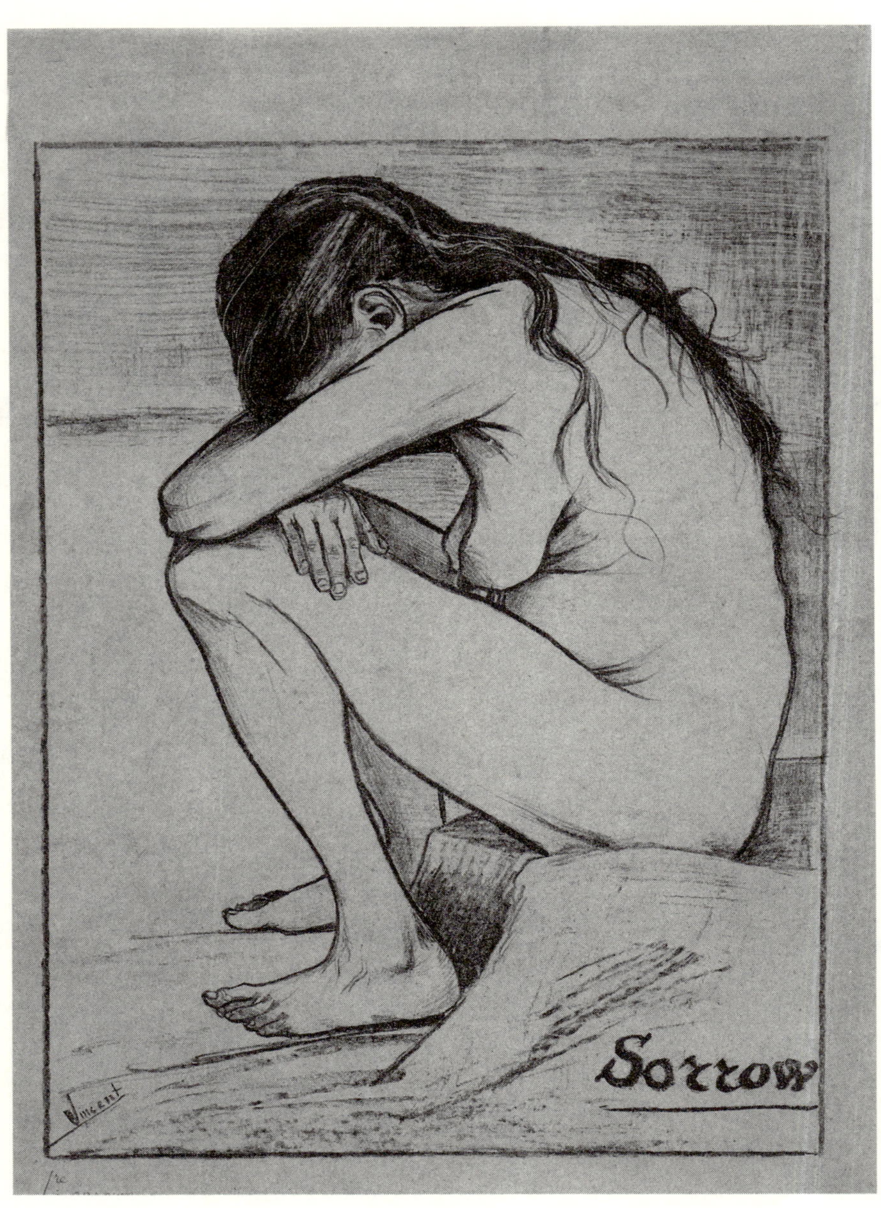

PLATE # 10

Sorrow

Van Gogh Museum, Amsterdam
(Vincent van Gogh Foundation)

SORROW

. . . most important is not to deceive or desert a woman . . . when she has fallen down.

My carpenter pencil draws
Sien as Mary Magdalen,
the paper receiving the void
between the rock and her thigh,
her lumbering breasts.

She sits for so long,
the sun goes down over the river.

If she were forgiven
what she did for bread;
her back bent over
from carrying the cross,
instead of a child,
she would not be invisible.

Light caresses her long hair
tangled into brambles.
At the foot of love's mean grave
I will scatter lilies of the valley.

NUDE WOMAN RECLINING SEEN FROM THE BACK

I imagine your hand
draped at the round of your breast,
your chestnut hair, unbraided,
your belly plumped
with my child.

Should you lift your eyes
toward the bedroom curtain
brushed with white rain,
you will see me there.

SELF-PORTRAIT WITH BANDAGED EAR

. . . my room full of canvases . . . nothing to send to the gallery when Gauguin sends his.

I try to paint myself serene
in a coat of marram grass,
my eyes, clear as a lake,
my hat, one hundred sable brushes.

Our arguments are terribly electric. . . we come out of them,
our heads exhausted as used batteries.

Unfinished paintings
on the wall, on the floor.
My face, fever green,
my heart in a sling.

MARGUERITE GACHET IN HER GARDEN

Pale maiden,
let me tender you, a yellow rose.

What has faded will return
turquoise to your eyes.

Your father keeps you,
overgrown.

Open the fence. Lift the hem
of your ribboned gown.

I wait under the cypress
to finish your lips in red berries.

VASE WITH AUTUMN ASTERS

. . . women in the twilight, women often already over thirty, up to fifty, such a dim, mysterious corner.

A shadow settles behind the vase,
its tight waist, the rounded hips.

Stems beginning their bend.
Overripe rouged petals

press against each other –
a mournful humming.

The women I have loved
grow old in separate rooms;

white blooms twirling across the floor,
my ageless brides.

LANDSCAPE WITH COUPLE WALKING AND CRESCENT MOON

At first there was only the cold purple mountain,
high above it, a sinister yellow moon uncurling.
The trees came next, low and billowed like clouds.

I took a step back. Then I painted myself into the landscape,
my pants, my smock, violet as the mountain.
I was cold and lonely. Loneliness does not have form.
So from my olive-toned skin, I painted in a woman.

Her hair is raven. I drape her in gold, color of the wheat field.
The woman and I are not yet lovers. Moving side by side,
I feel the promise of her hip. The hills are on fire,
my beard, on fire. The sky over the mountain bed erupts into flame.

OLIVE GROVE

A frenzy in the leaves,
fusion of turquoise and violet;
strokes not quite merging,
wood rubs against wood –
    hips
    buttocks
    breasts
Women arching their backs,
Men diving
head first
into their mouths,
black hair in the hollow
of the bark.
The brush cries "no more."
Beneath, a river
overflowing with semen
and blood.

DESCENT

The exhibitions, the picture stores, everything, everything, are in the clutches of fellows who intercept all the money…

And those high prices paid for work of painters who are dead, a kind of tulip trade, under which the living painters suffer.

WINTER GARDEN

Death takes hold
of my pen,
bundles itself up
beneath the naked
poplars.

Wrapped in straw
  the saplings,
  candles
  spinning

at death's back.

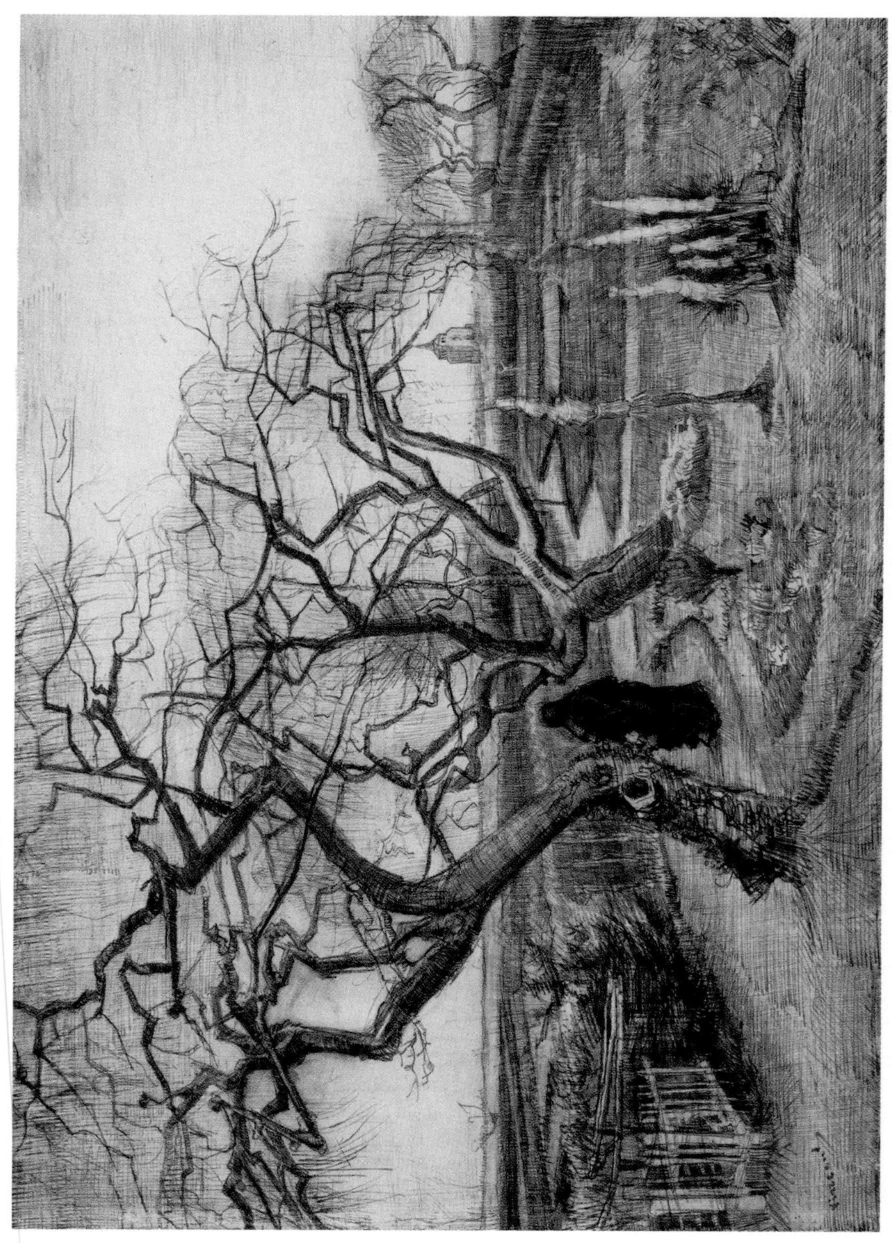

PLATE # 11

Winter Garden

Van Gogh Museum, Amsterdam
(Vincent van Gogh Foundation)

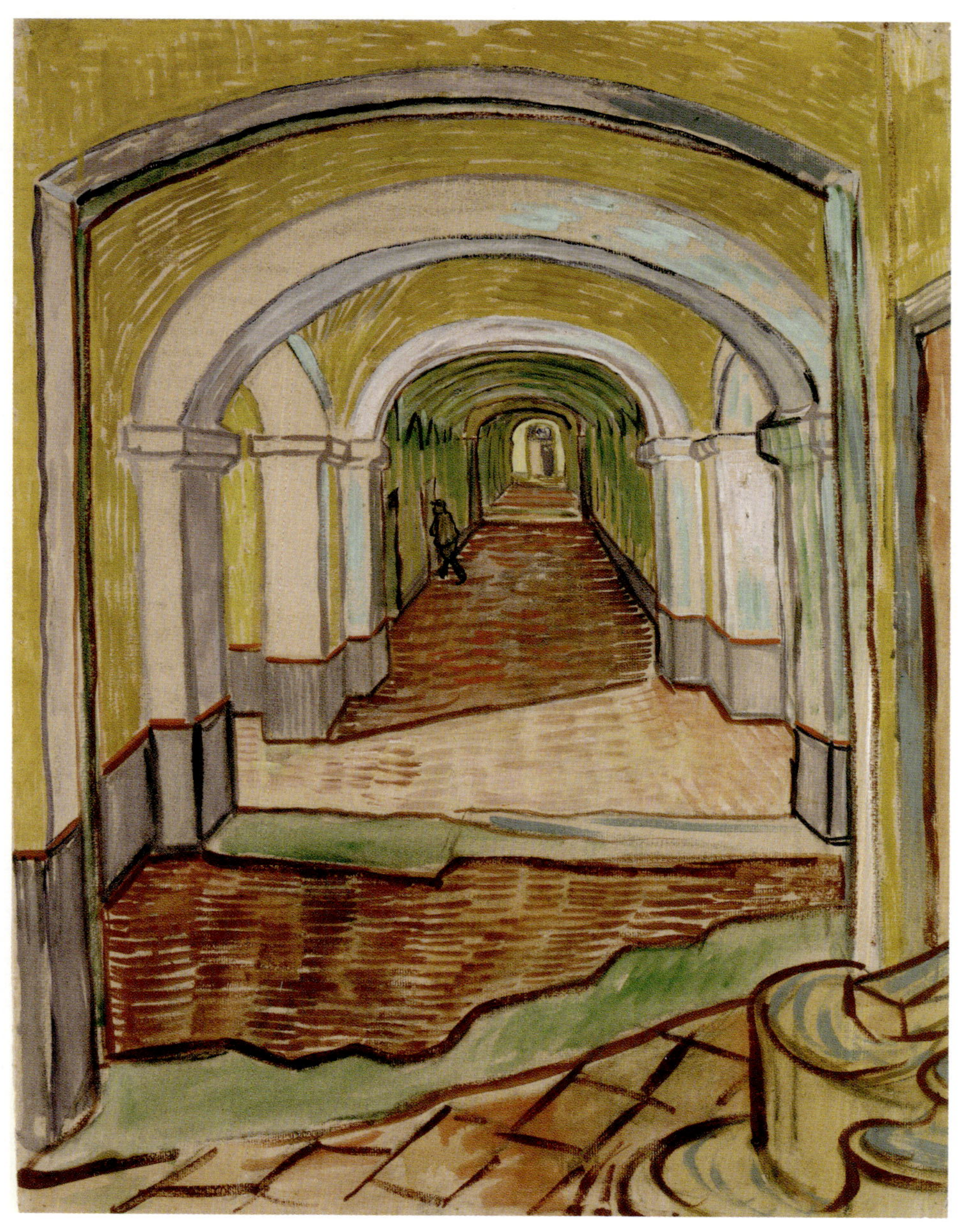

PLATE # 12

Corridor in the Asylum

Bequest of Abby Aldrich Rockefeller
1948 (48.190.2) Photograph © 1998
The Metropolitan Museum of Art

CORRIDOR IN THE ASYLUM

They feed us chickpeas and lentils, in fixed quantities and at regular intervals.

In the men's ward,
the archway yawns
tarnished gold.
Classical pillars,
squares aligned
at the base of the baluster.

Color breaks out:
turquoise, cinnamon.
My boots track red
down the corridor,
a tunnel,
lines
dizzying the floor.
I have lost the staircase

to my studio.
I walk into mirrorless walls.
Imagine a room
never leaving.

GARDEN OF SAINT-PAUL HOSPITAL

In the maniacal garden,
a bruised sky presses down.
The naked man
flapping his arms in a tree.
Upheaval below ground;
all the roots, drowning.
I rush back
through my green window.

TREE-ROOTS

Roots and ganglia.
The forest, upside down.
Serpents possessing the trees.

To placate myself,
I lay on tawny gold.
"Too late," the leaves hiss.

Black line, sienna line,
blue gone berserk.
The poplars fracture —
unclaimed bones.

EARS OF WHEAT

I paint my way through the curtain,
pale undulating wheat,
wisps of goldenrod;
depending on light's angle
in the field,
snakes or nightingales' necks.

Were it not for blackened lines,
the chaff would float
my body.

The sin of anonymity.
Tendrils,
fetal leaves.
Moths sounding
their white bells.

SELF-PORTRAIT

My face is a field overgrown with wild grasses.

Rows of dried stalks and ochre weeds.

Not the kind of field you lie down in.

Late autumn. I am leaf-veined, aging.

Red ignites my beard. Red that sizzles.

The way witches burn, I burn.

SELF-PORTRAIT WITH FELT HAT

The best way to treat a death is to swallow the illustrious dead.

Sunset rusts my beard;
my eyes, usurped by line.
My head is crowned with stone.

By my own hand,
I am dissolving
to blue
midnight.

VILLAGE STREET IN AUVERS

A child's palette,
purple finger paint, streaks and dashes
across a pinkened sky.

Rearing from the trees,
two black dragons.
I redden the primitive rooftops.

All my color, used up.
The more I shrink the road,
the more I prepare to let go.

UNDERGROWTH WITH TWO FIGURES

A woman and a man in the tall sweet grass.
She is a figment, he, a scarecrow.

The mauve trees multiply,
blackening the sky.
I lay down my brushes,

step into the wildflowers:
A thousand yellow butterflies whispering
hush now, hush.

*TWO CUT SUNFLOWERS**

The sun splits open:
blood seeds
gilded filaments
tattered yellow wings.

I spiral
into God's
greensick eye.

"...the shot...rang out on 27 July behind the chateau in Auvers...Van Gogh was buried in a sunny spot among the wheat fields...the coffin, covered with yellow flowers."

– Ronald de Leeuw, *The Letters of Vincent van Gogh*

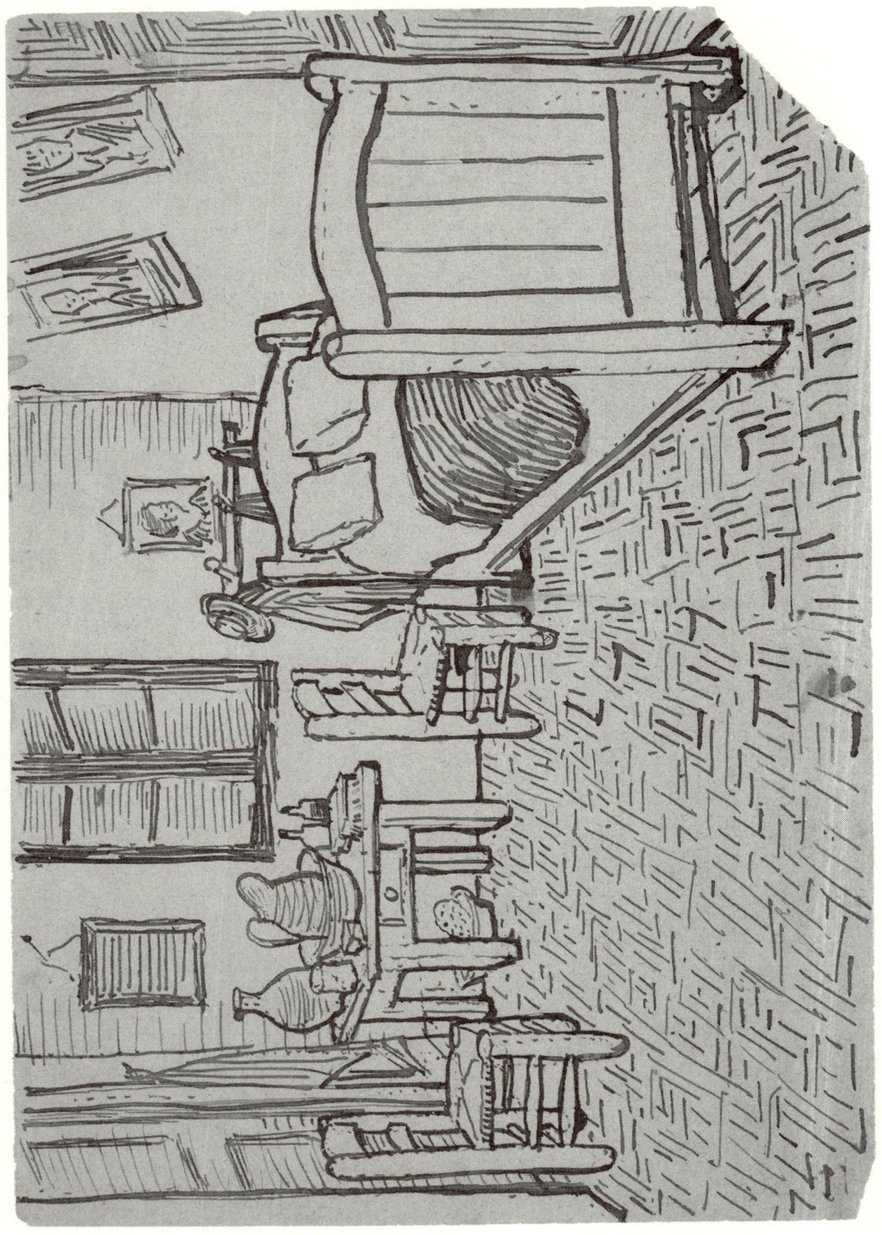

PLATE # 13

Sketch of Vincent's Bedroom in Arles

Van Gogh Museum, Amsterdam
(Vincent van Gogh Foundation)

THE BEDROOM

My limp smock.
Crooked portraits.
Lines in the floor moving
the dwarf chairs.

I will take to my bed,
dream in another language:
vermillion.
My coverlet spilling its form.
Red with a tongue,
she-devil red.

N A T U R E

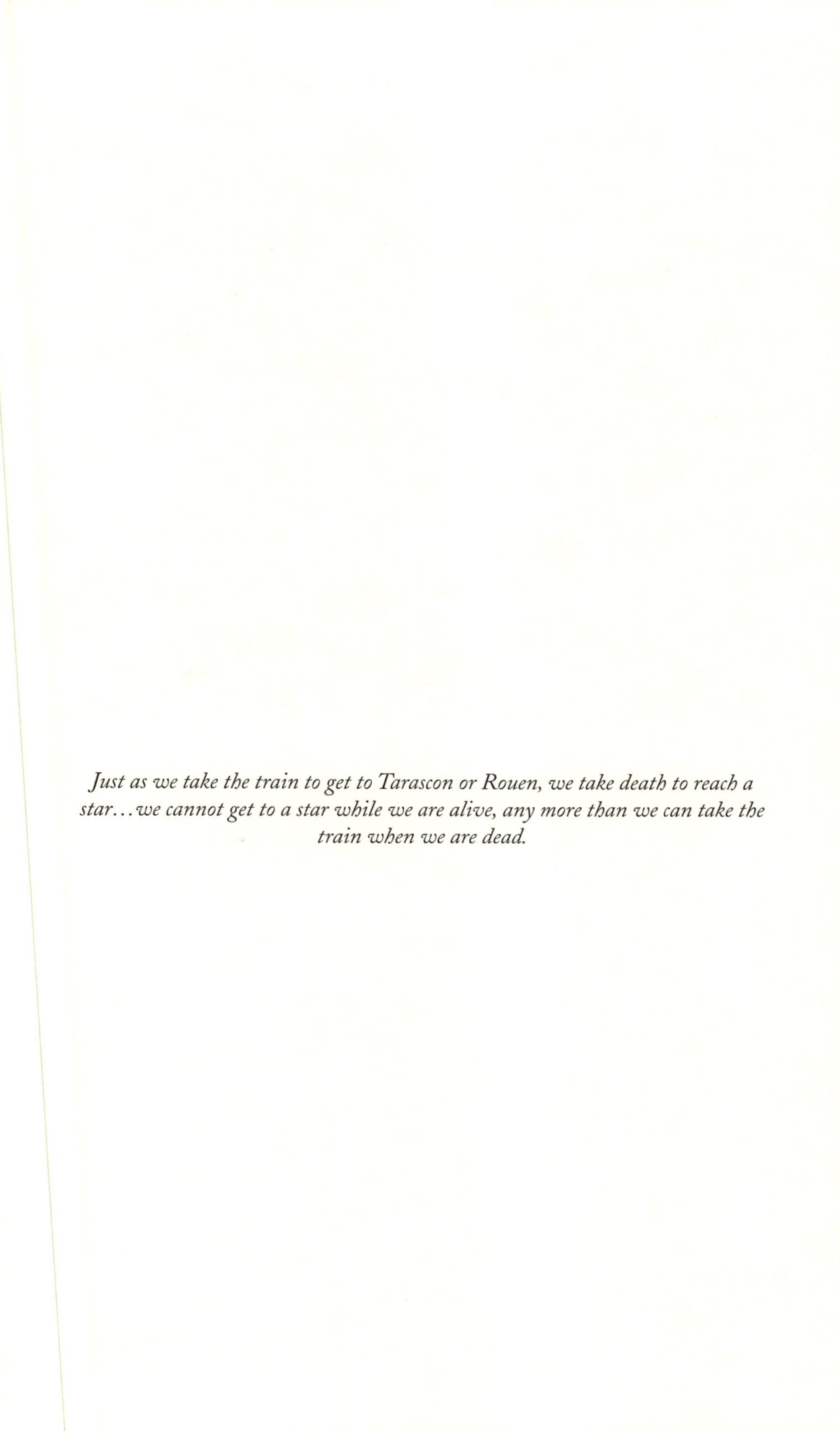

Just as we take the train to get to Tarascon or Rouen, we take death to reach a star…we cannot get to a star while we are alive, any more than we can take the train when we are dead.

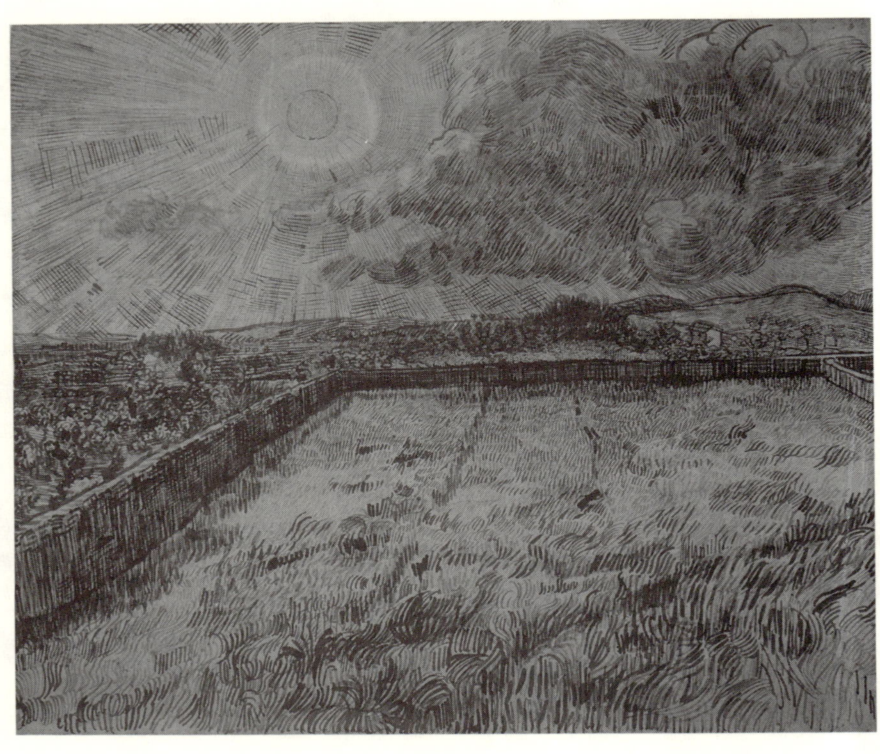

PLATE # 14

Wheatfield with Sun and Clouds

Collection Kröller-Müller Museum,
Otterlo, The Netherlands

WHEATFIELD WITH SUN AND CLOUDS

A train,
the confining wall,

moves my unsold canvases
beyond the field.

The clouds open
their fists.

In the heatless, pale
eye of the sun,

a turning to citron
I travel through.

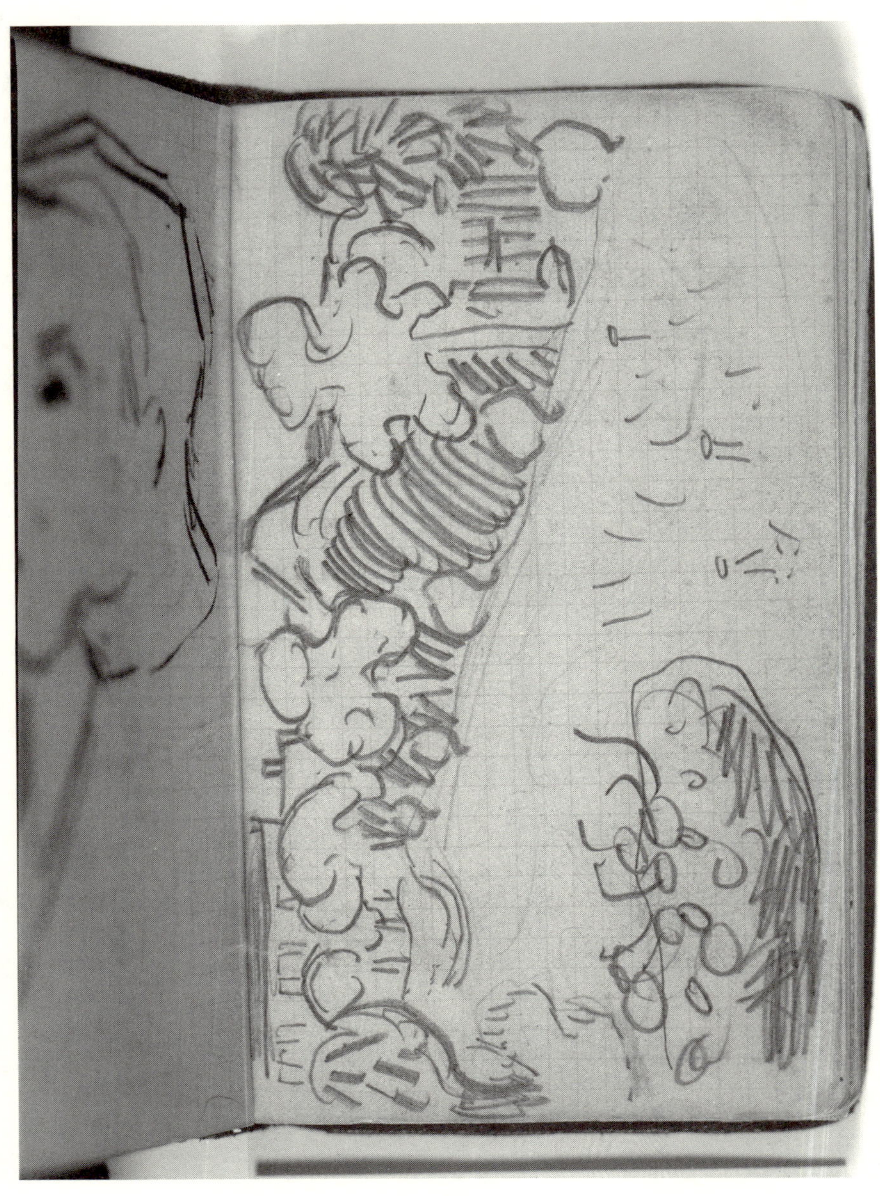

PLATE # 15

Sketch of Daubigny's Garden

Van Gogh Museum, Amsterdam
(Vincent van Gogh Foundation)

DAUBIGNY'S GARDEN

In my sketchbook,
intimate as skin,
I draw an island of roses.

Tree-clouds looming
near the edge of grass,
apostles at the last table.

Shadows pool
the margin.

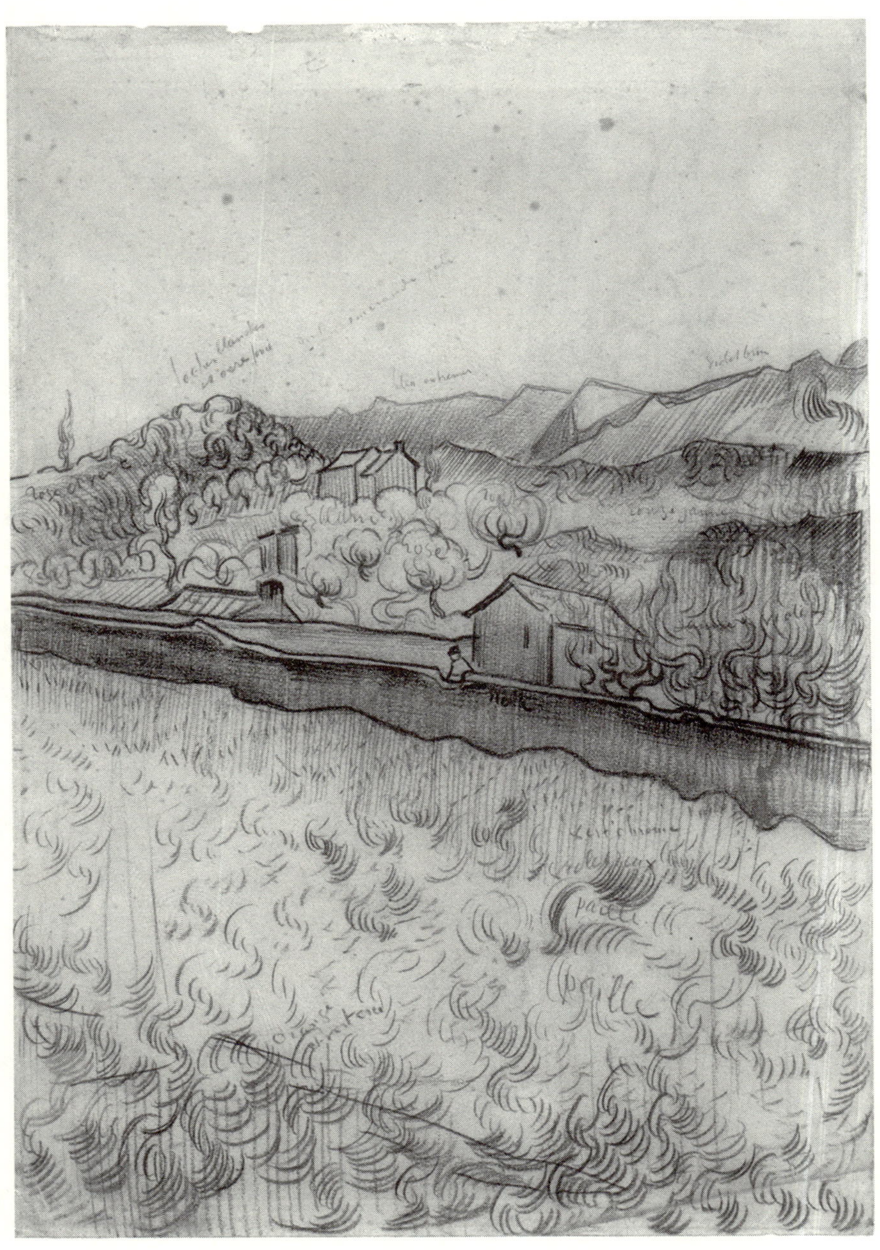

PLATE # 16

Mountain Landscape Behind the Walled Wheatfield

Van Gogh Museum, Amsterdam
(Vincent van Gogh Foundation)

MOUNTAIN LANDSCAPE BEHIND THE WALLED WHEATFIELD

From the asylum, notes to myself:

Nearest hills, capped with violet,
distant mountains, violet-brown.

Orange, chartreuse: words, lines
weaving in the wheat stalks.

White will billow
the almond trees.

Edged in black,
the enclosing wall.

No matter what color
I mark it,
the sky escapes me.

*BLOSSOMING CHESTNUT BRANCHES**

The month before I die,
whitened chestnut blossoms
trill through the branches.

The usual red,
insinuating itself
among the fewest petals.

Leaves in Auvers
press open their palms.

Overnight,
a loss of equilibrium;
from a corner,
shadows striate the undersides
of leaves.

I let my smock fall,
remake the sky violet-blue.
Wet paint
drips in rivulets,
discoloring the blooms.

**In February 2008, this painting, stolen from a gallery in Zurich, Switzerland, was discovered weeks later in an unlocked car that had been abandoned in front of a psychiatric hospital.*

WOMAN SEWING

Light from the field
enters the low window,
winding itself
around her tired sleeve.

Later, I re-paint her
worn bonnet,
the peat-stained apron,
the weight of her
hands woodening
as if she were making
her own shroud.

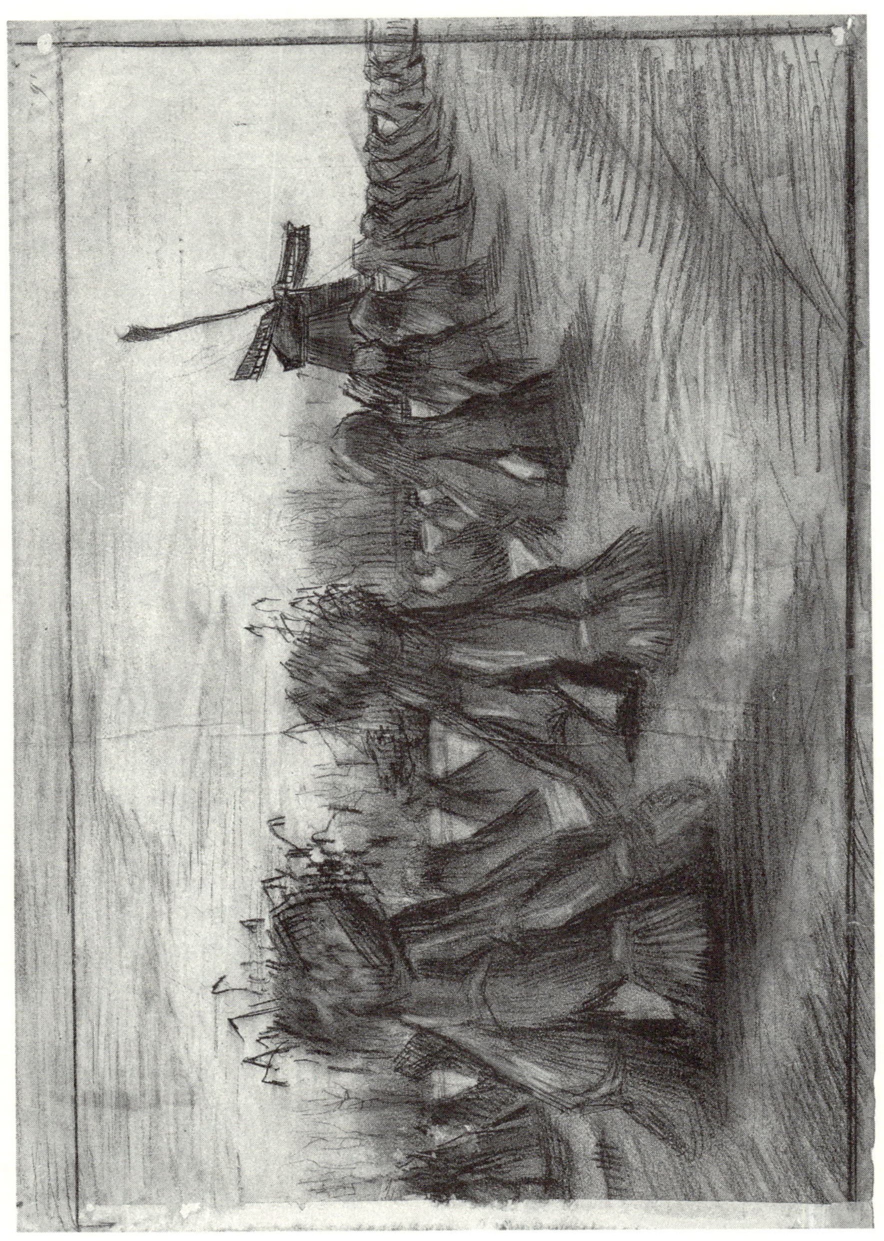

PLATE # 17

Stooks and a Mill

Van Gogh Museum, Amsterdam
(Vincent van Gogh Foundation)

STOOKS AND A MILL

Like peasants
bundled in mourning shawls,
walking a slow line
toward the grinding mill,
the clogs disappear
in the ground,
stitched like a wound.

THE RED VINEYARD

Sun licks the grass. The peasants, blue birds
gathering at the river. I layer rose madder
and sienna; the leaves elude me.
The idea of a harvest,

not the harvest: Light
turning red, then a violet rush,
earth, the grapes after rain.

To mock my failure, I should leave
the canvas empty.

LA CHARCUTERIE

Spring inside,
outside my rented room
above the smoky restaurant.
Succulent orange light,
the curtain, striped like wind
through the waves
at Saintes-Maries-de-la-Mer.
Across the street
moves through my window:
cobblestones, eggs multiplying;
the woman is a parrot
with emerald wings.

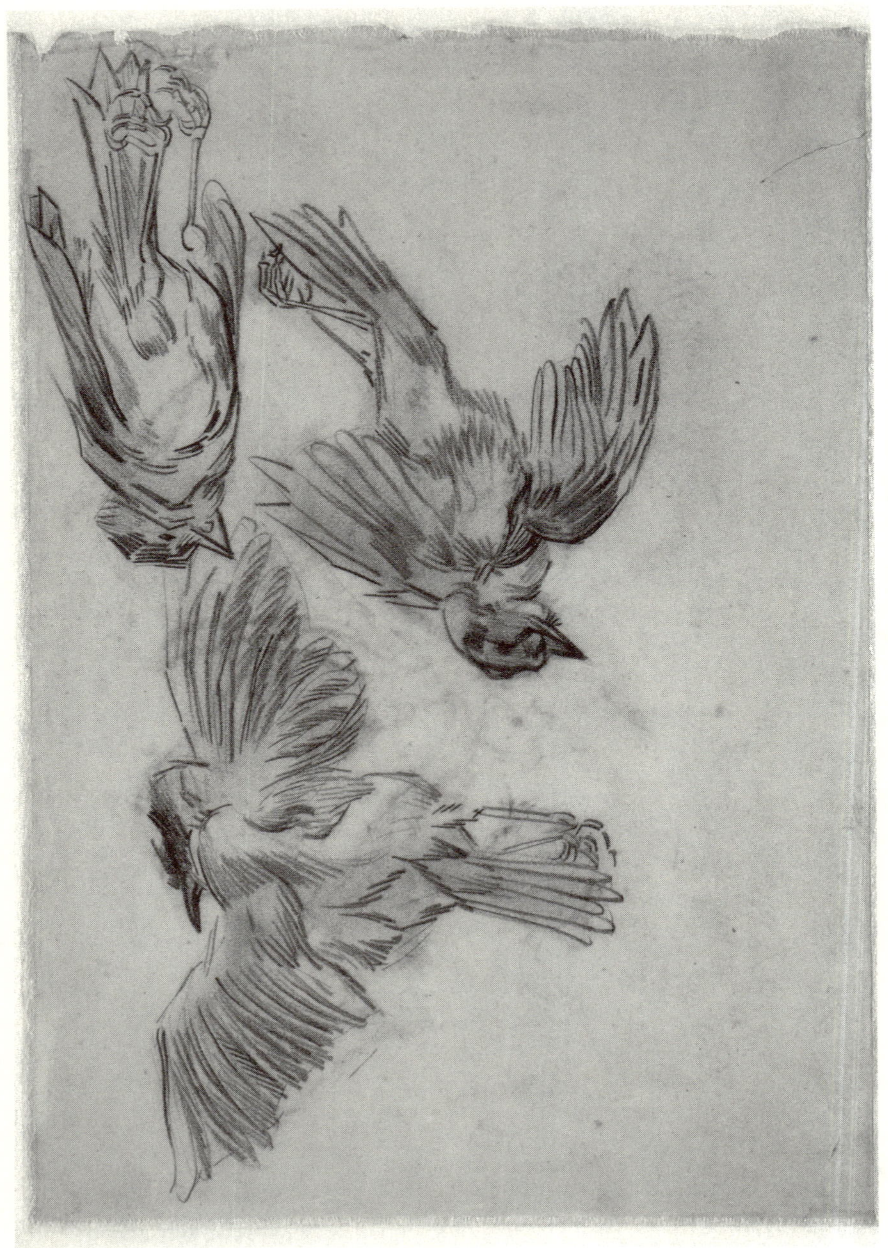

PLATE # 18

Studies of a Dead Sparrow

Van Gogh Museum, Amsterdam
(Vincent van Gogh Foundation)

STUDIES OF A DEAD SPARROW

Bowed head.
An old man's skinny legs.

Feathers extend
in pleated air.

Sleeping wings,
aflutter.

POET'S GARDEN

1.

Wild lace like fireflies
ignites the tall grass.

Verdant cedar shrub,
a perfect round.

In autumnal gold,
the ecstatic cypress

reaches toward the sky,
moving like a river,

affixed in layers
of citron.

2.

Red shadow climbs the trunks
of weeping ash.

At the horizon, the spire,
a silver thumbprint.

Windblown oleander,
white blossoms holding on.

Words, lamenting
their own loss,

escape
before the poem finishes.

*SCHEVENINGEN BEACH IN STORMY WEATHER**

Vengeful waves.
Whitecaps, the color of parchment.

Sand flying
into my eyes
and the wet paint.
Sea scrapes the dunes
to violet, green.
My feet misstep;
the beach grass, trampled wheat.

A trumpeter hovers
in the low mauve sky:
Fishermen are lost;
on shore, widows mourn
the ghost ship,
its bloody flag.

**In December of 2002, thieves broke through the glass ceiling of the Vincent van Gogh Museum, Amsterdam, and stole this painting. It is still missing.*

DIALOGUE

It is the same with people as with wheat; in the end you are ground down between the millstones to become bread.

I sketch the sower's open hand, his dead naked back.

I try to recover like a man who meant to commit suicide and, finding the water too cold, tries to regain the bank.

What keeps me is color thawing, white to violet blue.

Painting is a faith…

I imagine the Last Supper, the peasants, apostles turning toward him. Someone cuts a potato; someone holds the offering. The cottage walls darken. I retouch the faces with lamplight and smoke.

a memory.

Dearest brother, we will meet again. I spit my broken teeth out as stars.

ACKNOWLEDGMENTS

I especially wish to thank the editors of the following publications in which many of these poems or their versions first appeared:

Alehouse: "Corridor in the Asylum"

The Bitter Oleander: "Blooming Chestnut Branches," "Self-Portraits," "La Charcuterie," "Garden of Saint-Paul Hospital," "Ears of Wheat," "Dialogue," "Woman Sewing," "Avenue of Poplars at Sunset," "Two Cut Sunflowers," "Olive Grove," "The Red Vineyard," "Landscape with Couple Walking and Crescent Moon"

Boulevard: "Vase with Autumn Asters," "Tree-Roots," "Scheveningen Beach in Stormy Weather"

Salamander: "Undergrowth with Two Figures"

All quotations by Vincent van Gogh were respectfully culled from *The Complete Letters of Vincent van Gogh* (Thames & Hudson, Ltd., 1958) and *Dear Theo: The Autobiography of Vincent van Gogh* (Plume Books, 1937. Edited by Irving Stone.)

AFTERWORD

In 1880, when Vincent van Gogh started to make drawings, nothing suggested that he would be a success. Van Gogh did not go to an Academy of Fine Arts to be trained but decided to educate himself with the use of manuals on perspective and anatomy, and by asking for advice from artists with established reputations. His first drawings after nature are quite stiff and clumsy. A surprising exception is the drawing *The Bearers of the Burden* (1881). The hard life of workmen and farmers became an important motif in Van Gogh's oeuvre. Another example of this theme is the naked woman in *Sorrow* (1882), posed for by Sien Hoornik,with whom he lived briefly. The last years of his life in Holland, Van Gogh stayed with his parents in Nuenen. There, too, he rendered the life of ordinary people, like weavers at their looms and a farmer's family at dinner (*The Potato Eaters*, 1885). He also displayed his special gift for drawing landscapes. Confined by the rural surroundings of Nuenen, Van Gogh sought the cultural and commercial possibilities of city life. He moved to Paris, into the apartment of his brother Theo, who had been supporting him financially since his decision to become an artist. In Paris, Van Gogh saw the colorful paintings by the Impressionists for the first time and became friends with avant-garde artists like Henri de Toulouse-Lautrec, Paul Signac and Paul Gauguin. Their work influenced the style in which Van Gogh painted his landscapes, city views, still lifes and self-portraits (*Self-Portraits*, 1887). After living in Paris for two years, Van Gogh longed for the peace and quiet of the countryside. He left for Arles in the South of France, where he attained his own personal style. Among the paintings and drawings he made there are many masterpieces, including *The Bedroom* (1888). Within a year, Van Gogh suffered from the first attack of his illness, which soon would make it impossible to live independently. He was admitted to a mental hospital in Saint-Rémy, not far from Arles. Whenever possible, he made impressive drawings and paintings of the landscapes surrounding the asylum (*Wild Vegetation*, 1889). If his health prohibited him from working outside, he drew the interior (*Corridor in the Clinic*, 1889) or the view from his bedroom (*Mountain Landscape Behind the Walled

Wheatfield, 1890). After a year in the asylum, Van Gogh longed to be closer to his brother Theo and left for Auvers-sur-Oise, a village near Paris. Many artists preceded him there, among them the Barbizon artist Daubigny, whom Van Gogh greatly admired (*Daubigny's Garden*, 1890). Van Gogh was extremely productive in the couple of months he worked in Auvers. Unfortunately, this new energy did not go hand in hand with a positive state of mind. On the contrary, he felt very somber about the future. He died of a self-inflicted gunshot wound on 29 July 1890.

Marije Vellekoop
Curator of Prints and Drawings
Van Gogh Museum

Carol Dine is the author of two books of poetry and a memoir, *Places in the Bone* (Rutgers University Press, 2005). Her work is widely published in literary magazines, including *Blue Mesa Review, Boulevard,* and *Salamander*. She received the 2001 Frances Locke Memorial Poetry Award from the Bitter Oleander Press and the Sword of Hope Award for writing from the American Cancer Society. Her essay entitled "Layers," a reflection on art and September 11th, appears in the anthology *To Mend the World* (White Pine Press, 2002). Dine has been poet-in-residence at the MacDowell Colony, Yaddo, Ragdale, and the Wurlitzer Foundation. She teaches creative writing and writing on art at Suffolk University and lives in Boston, MA.